Then Winter

Then
Winter

poems by

Chloe Honum

BULL★CITY
PRESS

DURHAM, NORTH CAROLINA

THEN WINTER

Published in the United States of America

Library of Congress Cataloging-in-Publication Data

Honum, Chloe
Then Winter: poems / by Chloe Honum
p. cm.
ISBN-13: 978-1-4951-5765-3

Book design by Flying Hand Studio

Published by
BULL CITY PRESS
1217 Odyssey Drive
Durham, NC 27713

www.BullCityPress.com

ACKNOWLEDGMENTS

For their encouragement, I would like to thank the editors of the following journals, in which these poems, sometimes in different forms, first appeared:

32 Poems: "The Motel"

Alaska Quarterly Review: "Rest"

Copper Nickel: "The Ward Above"

Crazyhorse: "The Master of Dreams" (as "Exhaustion in the Psychiatric Ward")

Day One: "Blossoms in the Psychiatric Ward"

diode: "At America's Best Value Inn in Crossett, Arkansas" and "Teaching Poetry at the Juvenile Detention Center in Fayetteville, Arkansas"

Harvard Review Online: "On the Stairs Outside the Psychiatric Ward"

Hotel Amerika: "First Day of Partial Hospitalization," "Note Home," and "We're Supposed to Get Snow Tonight"

Linebreak: "Offerings"

One Throne: "Kiwi"

Salamander: "Phoebe"

The Southern Review: "Before Group Meditation" (as "Before Group Meditation in the Psychiatric Ward") and "The Angel"

storySouth: "Early Winter in the Psychiatric Ward"

Two Peach: "April in the Berkshires" (as "Breakdown in April") and "Stay Beside Me"

The Volta: "Late Afternoon in the Psychiatric Ward."

Waxwing: "Group Therapy" (as "Group Therapy in the Psychiatric Ward") and "Lunch Break in the Psychiatric Ward"

"The Angel" is written after the poem "Man and Camel," by Mark Strand.

My deep thanks to Grace Bonner, Lisa Fay Coutley, Dennis Covington, Donna Fleming, Marie Elena Foti, Rebecca Gayle Howell, Anna Kelly, Meaghan Mulholland, John Poch, Emily Pulfer-Terino, and Ariadne Thompson, for their true-blue friendship and wisdom.

Thank you to Ross White for his faith in this book.

For essential gifts of support, time, and encouragement, my thanks to Baylor University, the Djerassi Resident Artists Program, the Kerouac Project of Orlando, PEN Center USA, the Poetry Foundation, the Sewanee Writers' Conference, and the Texas Institute of Letters.

With endless gratitude to my family, Lainey Booth and Stefan Honum, and in memory, always, of Elaine Anderson.

My forever thanks to Jacob Shores-Argüello, for love and laughter.

These poems are for my mother, Pamela Honum.

CONTENTS

The Angel

On the eve of my thirteenth birthday, I found her in an alley. Her wings were crossed at violent angles. She was naked and her bruises were so bright that I ran my finger along them to check if the skin was broken. I bathed and clothed her. The garment fell apart on her body, like silk floating down and severing itself on a sword. Since then, she has gone everywhere with me. Occasionally, people see her and startle. They ask her if she's all right, but she speaks only to me, as if I were the translator of her ancient, mottled language.

April in the Berkshires

Alone in my bedroom, I sob,
and the wardrobe steps forward,
like a coffin-mother, to embrace me.

Later, standing at the back door,
a coyote crosses my vision
on a wave of snow. This

is intimacy: once, in a supermarket,
you slid up behind me,
covered my eyes, and said, *guess who?*

Did I recognize your touch or your voice?
I sleep with the windows open
and the rain climbs into my bed

like a lover, naked beneath the quilt.
I could roll over and wrap
my arms around the rain.

On the Stairs Outside the Psychiatric Ward

I stand with the boy with the twisted body
while the smoke from his cigarette signs its slow signature.
He leans on his cane and the cane shakes.
It is late afternoon, almost dark.

We are day patients and soon will go home.
The boy says, *I got into some trouble in Texas,*
which is so far away it doesn't seem to exist,
not with what's going on now.

All around us autumn is throwing
gold and crimson leaves into the street
while starlings are holding tight on a telephone wire,
heads tucked in the cold. And the boy

and the Vietnam vet, who has just joined us,
and I are looking up with yearning, as though
we could solve that string of bird and sky arithmetic
and know the ages of our souls.

First Day of Partial Hospitalization

The windows in the common room look down on a parking lot. Snow keeps coming, though it is already the conqueror of anything it wants. When a baby is born, a speaker mounted above the entrance plays a lullaby. One patient wonders aloud why music doesn't play when somebody dies, suggests "Stairway to Heaven." On my drive home, trucks swallow the narrow hills. I all but close my eyes. Hurry, darling. I would side with winter—if it would free me, I would stay.

Lunch Break at the Psychiatric Ward

The fluorescent light is covering me like a hood of silk. It smells of sweat and medicine. The fish tank in the hallway is a risk and a gesture. A box of wonder—we are trusted not to throw ourselves against it.

*

Once, when I was small, my mother lay on the carpet and asked me to walk barefoot up her back. I grew very light, hovering above myself, and made the journey. I had to balance my distance from her body. When she rolled over, my feet became birds in the golden leaves of her hair.

*

Outside, the boy with the twisted body is leaning on his cane and smoking a cigarette. The sky, the snow, and the smoke pass gray, white, and silver around in a circle. In an hour we will go back inside the building. We'll climb the narrow stairs, as if venturing into the attics of our lives.

Note Home

Mother, you have never seen such snow, such emphasis on setting. So it is accurate to say my heart broke in the snow. One patient here is a Vietnam vet. His torso is hard like an old-fashioned suitcase. *Kick my dog*, he says, referring to his beloved animal over ten years dead, and *I'll kick your ass*. The light is fluorescent. Everything hums. It is so important to go on naming, even if all I said to you this winter was *snow, snow, snow*.

Offerings

I have saved my pantomime of the sky for you. Let me lie with my head in your lap. I will sing the song of the trees in the cold wind, the way they rush up like flames, their leaves rippling. I want to show you everything you might have missed. With my fingers I will emulate moonlight resting on a field of violets. I am about as convincing as the child playing the sun in the school recital. But I have rain in my hair. This much is true. Let me bring it to you.

Late Afternoon in the Psychiatric Ward

The fluorescent light
goes off and the shadows
fall apart like a cardboard fort.

The invisible should be sturdier,
like that stormy summer
the rain came so heavy

the waterfall was just
a thicker column of sky.
Now a fly throws itself

down on the formica table
and buzzes and spins
on its back, quickening

the poison. It resembles
a word scribbled out.
Won't do, won't do.

But oh you of the river-
wet lips, I miss you
this moment, and this.

Stay Beside Me

The psychiatric ward has three levels. We are the day patients, and above us are the overnighters. Above them are those in the most danger. In the common room, the Vietnam vet tells me that his father, the fire chief, molested his sisters. When he says, *my sisters*, his slow, gravelly voice rises. Then he falls silent. I think he is afraid to be womanly. But in the shade beneath his ball cap, the word *sisters* keeps rising, like the moon above a beach where dolphins have mistaken its light for a shared mind, and are swimming in with the waves.

The Ward Above

I don't need to look up to know that inside some of the fluorescent lights there are dead flies on their backs, their wings at crisp diagonals. The psychiatrist has a face like an old dictionary. I imagine myself in the ward above, for the more severe cases. I'm afraid I'll float up and ask to be admitted. In the common room, the Vietnam vet says, *No, you don't want to go up there.* Everything he says, he says again with his eyes. At home, my dog sleeps beside me. She groans as I slide my hand beneath her head. I speak to her. I carry her warm, happy skull through the night.

We're Supposed to Get Snow Tonight

One patient among us has had shock therapy. I ask if it helped and she shrugs both shoulders. Staring at the floor, she says, *I think it does affect the memory.* One patient wears the softest clothes. Even her boots are soft. She says, *It's a good day if I get to see him,* as she drifts across the room. During our lunch break, I drive into town. The hills roll fast then slow, keeping pace with a crow arcing overhead. I buy a latte, wrap my hands around the paper cup, and hold still for a moment on the sidewalk. Coming toward me, a hooded woman carries a gladiola like a spine in bloom. She passes without raising her eyes. And the wind grows colder.

Blossoms in the Psychiatric Ward

One patient among us suspects we're actors in a play. He is a gentle interrogator, and moves slowly around the common room. Between questions, he folds and refolds his handkerchief. I have seen his face before in heavy, browning blossoms, ancient and disorganized. The counselor asks, *And you, too? Are you also an actor?* The man nods then shakes his head. His eyes are apologetic. Beyond the window, there's a pause in the rain. Something shimmering and tear-streaked begins to turn, though whether it's coming or leaving we can't say.

Group Therapy

The counselor is passing around a black, velvet sack filled with questions. *What is your idea of a perfect evening? Who is your biggest inspiration?* He's beaming, waiting for our answers. Beyond the window, autumn toys with ideas of heaven. The trees become fiercely talented and focused. Then winter.

*

Some say love, it is a river, I sang as a girl in school assembly. We sang standing up. I was ready to faint all that year. For five days each month, my blood came as bright as plum juice. When I finally fainted, it was as silky as I'd imagined, as if sleeping and waking were two sides of one pearl.

*

In any group, I want to know: Who's the mother? The boy with the twisted body, he's the angel. The Vietnam vet is the son. The nervous old lady is the baby. The counselor is the meddling neighbor. Now that I see a family, I can breathe. The leaves are crimson. I have something to tear down.

The Master of Dreams

By late afternoon, the master of dreams
is close beside me. I hand him his props.
I give him my scarf, the clingy texture

of a hibiscus, and pass him a ringing
phone that I don't want to answer.
Sometimes he takes things on his own.

In the common room, I drop an apple
and the master of dreams whisks it away
on a river of fluorescent light. Silent

and meticulous, he takes notes on the wind
and the falling crimson leaves. By evening,
he waits in a shimmering boat.

He comes from a place both deeper
and closer than nowhere,
though he has lived nowhere, too.

Early Winter in the Psychiatric Ward

The counselor plays his game of questions.
If you could live in any time period,
he asks us, *when would you live?*

Now, the manic boy answers, as though jumping
to the head of the queue to enter the present.
Not now, the Vietnam vet says,

it's too violent, and he talks about the late
Fifties, the Friday nights
dancing at the Showboat.

Outside, the rain comes to a feathery end.
The geese introduce themselves to dusk
with ragged cries. Winter at their backs,

they heave upward.
Their wings open like old, heavy books,
their stories veering into the wild.

Kiwi

The fluorescent light in the group therapy room is vetting me for some terrible migration. I ask the counselor to turn it off. My native bird is flightless. It's a cousin to the moa: a brown hut of a bird. The boy with the twisted body is talking and dabbing sweat from his brow with a handkerchief. The lights go off, and suddenly it's late afternoon and cloudy. The Vietnam vet says his violent father was the fire chief, and that's why no one believed his mother. He shakes his head and blinks. My native bird is nocturnal. Though it has lived fifty million years, it and the sky have reached no agreement.

Before Group Meditation

I recall splendor.
On a borrowed bicycle,
I wobbled fast

downhill over jutting roots,
a swarm of horseflies
like a grainy moon

following close behind.
At the bottom of the hill,
a little rain shining in

a corner of wind.
Now the upbeat counselor
passes around a basket

of rocks. My friend Dan,
the Vietnam vet, says,
I knew I wasn't going to be smart

so boy I was going to be tough.
All his sentences are like that,
clean as autumn. Each afternoon

we sit in a circle. I take a rock,
I wish you were here,
and I pass the basket on.

Rest

First one psychiatrist is gone, pulled away
on a tide of fluorescent light.
Then the other is gone too,
to tend to matters in the ward above.

In the common room, we talk about side effects,
night sweats and low libidos,
and about miracle drugs. *Like a light switch*,
one patient says, and we look longingly

beyond the window, at the birds
draped like strings of black pearls
around the saffron-colored trees.
The patient who thinks we're actors in a play

asks me questions about poetry.
Flowers freshly cut and wrapped in newspaper,
that's how I want to rest, my dreams
like white petals absorbing ink.

Phoebe

At the clinic, a nurse taps my veins and they find their tiny voices. Blood sweeps into the vial and a chunk of snow slides from my boot. The shine on the linoleum floor is brutal, but no one is saying so. Outside, it is both noon and evening, as if winter were trying to be giving. In the parking lot: a hooded woman. You want to know what I believe? I believe my dog would come between my death and me, that she would come huffing and shaking all over, as her dreams allow.

The Motel

On the outskirts of a thundering town,
I checked in. My hair was swingy with rain,
my umbrella blown inside out.
The cement stairs went up and up;

had they risen one flight higher
I might have slept in a palace of violet
and silver clouds. As it was, my room
was an ugly place to miss you from,

with thin carpet and curtains
that seemed to exhale dust.
Seeing myself in the speckled mirror,
I lay flat on the bed. In my hand was a map

of the motel on which the clerk
had circled my home for the night—
among a series of doors,
a blurry number inside a drop of rain.

At America's Best Value Inn in Crossett, Arkansas

The mist is the rain gone under cover at the end of summer.
    Standing on the iron fence around the swimming pool,
the pigeons have the gray sheen of underpaid men. Sparrows
    sing the night in question into question. Maybe sense is not a place
I want to linger, like the cement hallway that leads to the ice machine,
    the ground studded with old chewing gum. By my feet, two butterflies twirl
like fire that has lost its way. I find my room and close the door,
    a beige door bearing a stranger's—or many strangers'—inky fingerprints.
In the morning: a cool wind, the treetops tracing the letters of their private alphabet.
    In the distance: white clots of smoke rising from the Georgia-Pacific paper plant.
All those hot blank pages—who needs them? My phone could ring
    at any moment. You could say, _____. Mother Silence
could appear behind me, waving from any one of these dark windows.

Teaching Poetry at the Juvenile Detention Center in Fayetteville, Arkansas

It's cold and the light is blurry,
the fluorescents spasming,
the walls a steely gray.
Each child is given a pencil.

Their cells are just beyond
the heavy sliding doors.
They write get-away poems
and tree-house poems.

Sack of weed and siren poems.
A flea appears on my arm and
quivers, like a fleck of onyx.
I watch it bite and gleam and the boys

sitting across from me
watch it, too. In a cement
tomb, hope is anything
that travels in big leaps.

ABOUT THE AUTHOR

image: Victoria Marie Bee

CHLOE HONUM was raised in Auckland, New Zealand. She is the author of *The Tulip-Flame*, selected by Tracy K. Smith for the Cleveland State University Poetry Center First Book Prize. *The Tulip-Flame* was named a finalist for the 2015 PEN Center USA Literary Award, and won the 2014 Foreword Book of the Year Award and a Texas Institute of Letters Award. Chloe's poems have appeared in *The Southern Review*, *The Paris Review*, *Orion*, and elsewhere, and she has received a Ruth Lilly Fellowship and a Pushcart Prize. She is an assistant professor of English at Baylor University.

Find her online at http://chloehonum.com/.

ALSO FROM BULL CITY PRESS

LENA BERTONE, *Behind This Mirror*

TOMMYE BLOUNT, *What Are We Not For*

KATIE BOWLER, *State Street*

ELLEN C. BUSH, *Licorice*

ANDERS CARLSON-WEE, *Dynamite*

TIANA CLARK, *Equilibrium*

BEN HOFFMAN, *Together, Apart*

B.J. HOLLARS, *In Defense of Monsters*

ANNE KEEFE, *Lithopedia*

MICHAEL MARTONE, *Memoranda*

MICHAEL McFEE, *The Smallest Talk*

JILL OSIER, *Should Our Undoing Come Down Upon Us White*

EMILIA PHILLIPS, *Beneath the Ice Fish Like Souls Look Alike*

ANNA ROSS, *Figuring*

LISA GLUSKIN STONESTEEET, *The Greenhouse*

ANNE VALENTE, *An Elegy for Mathematics*

LAURA VAN DEN BERG, *There Will Be No More Good Nights Without Good Nights*

MATTHEW OLZMANN & ROSS WHITE, eds., *Another & Another: An Anthology from the Grind Daily Writing Series*